CHOSEN FO

Chosen For Glory

Robert Sheehan

Christian Focus Publications Ltd

Published by
Christian Focus Publications Ltd.
Tain   **Houston**
Ross-shire   **Texas**

© **1989 Christian Focus Publications Ltd.**
ISBN 0906 731 96 8

Christian Focus Publications is a non denominational publishing house. We publish
authors' books and the views expressed are those of the authors.

Contents

Preface

'God knows everything. God is sovereign. God has chosen His people. Therefore those who are to be saved, will be and so I need do nothing'.

The premise is true — it is our conclusion that is desperately wrong.

Many who come in contact with the Word of God give this excuse for inactivity. Sadly this is also an unspoken view of many Christians in relation to their unconverted friends and neighbours.

Robert Sheehan, in this book, deals clearly with this issue. We rejoice in the challenge of the book and in its constant appeal to Scripture.

Our prayer is that you will read it with God's help and that afterwards you will have a clear grasp of the two glorious doctrines of God's election and our responsibility.

W.H.M.M.

Section One
Election

Chapter 1

The Fact

A chosen people

Every Bible-believing Christian accepts that the Scriptures teach election, i.e. that God chooses to bless some people in a special way that He does not bless others. The most obvious example of such election is the Jewish people. They took great pride in being 'God's chosen people', and did so with considerable Biblical support. Did not Moses remind Israel, 'You are a holy people to the Lord your God: the Lord your God has chosen you to be a people for himself, a special treasure above all the peoples on the face of the earth'?[1]

Chosen servants

Similarly, few people would deny the fact that, as well as having had a chosen nation, God has chosen servants. There are many of them fulfilling various functions. The Levites were described as those, 'the LORD your God has chosen . . . out of all your tribes to stand to minister in the name of the LORD'. A King, like Saul, was presented to the people as, 'him whom the LORD has chosen'. In the New Testament also we are told that our Lord 'called his disciples to him; and from them he chose twelve whom he also named apostles'.[2]

It might be thought that all the references in Scripture to chosen people could be covered under either of these two heads, but it is not so. A third category of chosen people is also found.

Election within election

Whilst Israel as a nation is referred to as God's chosen people,[3] a distinction between the Israelites is also drawn in Scripture. Paul, in particular, develops this theme in Romans chapters nine to eleven.

Faced with Jewish rejection of Christ and a despising of her many privileges, Paul reminds us that, 'they are not all Israel who are of Israel'. To put that in another way, not all who are physically Jews, not all who outwardly belong to God's people, belong inwardly. Chosen Israel may be divided into two.[4]

As Paul develops his argument and discusses the rejection of unbelieving Judaism, he contends that God has not rejected all Jews. In every generation 'there is a remnant according to the election of grace'.[5] Always God preserves a portion of the chosen nation for Himself. These are the remnant and they are chosen by grace. Paul contrasts this remnant with the rest of Israel and calls them the elect. 'Israel has not obtained what it seeks; but the elect have obtained it and the rest were hardened'.[6]

We have then an election within an election. From the nations of the world, God chose or elected Israel for special privileges. Yet, only the elect remnant of the chosen nation obtained salvation. Only the election of grace obtained the righteousness that comes by faith in Christ.

In a similar way, not all those who were chosen to serve God were necessarily saved. The supreme example of this is Judas Iscariot. There is no doubt that he was chosen to serve: 'When it was day he called his disciples to him and from them he *chose* twelve whom he also named apostles: Simon ... and Judas Iscariot who also became a traitor'. Our Lord acknowledged, 'Did I not *choose* you, the twelve, and one of you is a devil'?[7]

As our Lord's death drew near, He was speaking to His disciples, having washed their feet, and promised blessing on their obedience. Suddenly, however, He says, 'I do not speak concerning all of you. I know whom I have *chosen*, but that the Scripture may be fulfilled, "He who eats bread with me had lifted up his heel against me" '.[8] In a room where our Lord was present only with his twelve apostles, whom He had chosen to serve Him, He draws a contrast between the eleven whom He had chosen and the twelfth. Obviously He is using 'chosen' in a different sense than He had in the earlier passages. Again we have elect disciples among the chosen apostles, those who are elect to salvation among those who are chosen to serve.

Conclusion

It is evident, therefore, that this third category of elect people exists. They are not simply elected to privilege or to service but to salvation. This is not merely an inferred teaching. It is explicitly stated. Paul writes to the Thessalonian Christians and contrasts them with the perishing world. He says,

'But we are bound to give thanks to God always for you, brethren beloved by the Lord, because God from the beginning chose you for salvation'.[9]

Similar phrases are used elsewhere to describe the same fact. 'God did not appoint us to wrath but to obtain salvation'. As many as had been appointed to eternal life believed'.[10] It is clear that if we are submissive to the teaching of the Bible we must accept the fact that there are people whom God has chosen and appointed to salvation.

For further thought

1. What does the case of Balaam teach us about the differences between serving God and being saved by God? (Numbers 22-24, 31; Joshua 13:22; 24:9-10; Nehemiah 13:2; Micah 6:5; 2 Peter 2:15; Jude 11; Revelation 2:14).
2. What are most important, a person's gifts or a person's graces? (Matthew 7:21f)

1. *Deuteronomy 7:6.*
2. *Deuteronomy 18:5; 1 Samuel 10:24; Luke 6:13.*
3. *Deuteronomy 7:6.*
4. *Romans 9:1-6 cf 2:28-29.*
5. *Romans 11:5.*
6. *Romans 11:7.*
7. *Luke 6:13,16; John 6:70.*
8. *John 13:7,18.*
9. *2 Thessalonians 2:13.*
10. *1 Thessalonians 5:9; Acts 13:48.*

Chapter 2

The Reason

Even among those who accept that God has chosen a people to salvation there remains a dispute concerning the reason for this election. Why has God chosen to save anyone? Is there something in man or in particular people that determines this choice or is there something in God?

Do men earn God's choice?

We must begin by asserting categorically that no-one deserves salvation. Both the Old and New Testaments unite in declaring human sinfulness and its desert. Even at such a high religious point as the dedication of the Temple, Solomon had to acknowledge, 'for there is no-one who does not sin'. Paul can survey humanity and declare that, 'there is none righteous, no not one ... there is none who does good, no not one ... all have sinned'. Sin does not merit salvation. It earns death as its wages, its just and fitting reward.[1] Human virtue does not exist when judged by God's standards. All is marred by sin and so cannot attract God and cause him to give salvation. God does not choose to save us because we are sinners! We deserve nothing from God but the penalty of our sins.

Is God obliged to save?

If man does not merit salvation, is the reason why God determines to save some because he is obliged to save? Is God under obligation to sinners? Do sinners have a right to be saved? Many people feel they do. They feel that God *must* provide salvation and offer it to all men or somehow leave himself open to criticism. This feeling has no Biblical support. In fact, just the opposite is taught.

Men are not the only ones of God's creatures who have sinned. There are angels who are also moral beings, who have sinned. The angels who sinned have never had any salvation planned, provided or held out for them. They were not spared but reserved for judgment.[2] Since their sin, their situation has been hopeless — and this is not considered in Scripture as compromising the love of God or contradictory to it.

If God can be love yet not obliged to offer sinful angels salvation, he can be under no obligation to provide salvation for sinners. Again it needs to be asserted that God is only *obliged* to give sin its wages — death.[3] No man or angel has a right to complain if he is left to reap the consequences of his sin.

Did God choose on the basis of faith foreseen?

Another popular idea is that God's choice of men to salvation is based upon His foresight of their faith. It is argued that He looked ahead in time, foresaw who would believe, and ordained them to salvation.

Supposed Scriptural support is found for this idea in the statement of Paul that God predestined whom He foreknew, and Peter's assertion that election is according to God's foreknowledge.[4]

There are, however, two serious objections to this view. Firstly, Paul does not write of *something* God foreknew, i.e. faith or virtue but *persons* — 'whom'.[5] If to foreknow is equivalent to foresee it would mean that all those whom God had foreseen were predestined to be made like God's Son. It is evident that God has complete knowledge of all things and all people,[6] and this would make Paul teach universal foreknowledge, predestination, calling, justification and glorification — an obvious absurdity in the light of Biblical teaching.

Secondly, to foreknow is not equivalent to foresee. Biblically speaking, the verb 'know' is a relationship verb. Adam 'knew' Eve and she conceived. Joseph did not 'know' Mary until she had given birth to our Lord.[7] In such cases the verb means to have sexual relations with, to be intimate, to have a relationship.

In its spiritual usage, the Scriptures retain the meaning of entering into or having an intimate relationship. Israel was marked out from the other nations for both privileges and responsibilities. She only was 'known' of all the families of the earth. In the same way Paul sees it as inconceivable that the Lord should reject His foreknown people.[8] To foreknow, far from meaning to foresee, means to forelove, to enter into a relationship, to be committed to a person beforehand.

Election according to foreknowledge is then not a choice made on the basis of foresight but a choice made out of a determination to love and enter into a relationship. God's foreknown people are fore-loved. This leads us to the real reason for God's election.

The free grace and sovereign purpose of God cause election

The Scriptures emphasise that when God chooses a man or woman to salvation, He is not moved to do so by human whim or effort. Nor is it because He compares two sinners to see which is good and which is bad and makes a choice between them. God's election has a purpose that is not based upon human goodness.[9]

God chooses to show mercy sovereignly, i.e. freely, as it pleased Him to show it. God has mercy on whom He wants to have mercy. His purpose in election is a purpose of grace, i.e. it does not give man what he deserves, it does not give out of obligation, but it gives and plans freely because it wants to. Paul reminds us that the electing, predes-tinating purposes of God are to the praise of His glorious grace. As Moses said to Israel of old, the Lord loved her because He loved her.[10] The reason for His electing love lay not in her but in Him. Robert Murray McCheyne correctly asserts, 'Chosen not for good in me'.

If we ask the questions, why did He love me, why did He choose me, why did He not leave me in my sin to my own desired fate? The answer is simply 'grace'. He loved because He loved. He chose because He showed grace. He purposed our salvation for no other reason than because He wanted to.

For further thought

1. How does Ezekiel 16:1-14 emphasise the pure grace of God's love?

2. How would you respond to the statement that there is nothing in the sinner to turn God's heart toward him but plenty to turn Him away?

1. 1 Kings 8:46; Romans 3:10,11,23; 6:23.
2. 2 Peter 2:4; Jude 6.
3. Romans 6:23.
4. Romans 8:29; 1 Peter 1:2.
5. Romans 8:29.
6. Psalm 139.
7. Genesis 4:1; Matthew 1:25.
8. Amos 3:1; Romans 11:2.
9. Romans 9:16,11; 2 Timothy 1:9.
10. Romans 9:18; 2 Timothy 1:9; Ephesians 1:4-6; Deuteronomy 7:7-8.

Chapter 3

The Means

There are those who assume that once we have grasped the doctrine of election we have said all that needs to be said about salvation. One man told me that he believed that God had His elect among the Jews, Hindus and Moslems and could not see the need for missionary work. The assumption of this man, and others like him, is that God's purpose of election is not fulfilled in history by the use of means. But Scripture teaches that it is! We are not chosen to salvation in a vacuum but through a number of means. These we will now consider.

Election in Christ

Paul reminds us that God chose us in Christ.[1] The doctrine of election does not make the work of Christ redundant. It is precisely because there is a people to save that Christ has come. Our Lord's name Jesus was given because 'He will save his people from their sins'. He is the Good Shepherd who 'gives his life for the sheep'. 'Christ loved the Church and gave himself for it'. Because the Father had given Him a people to save, our Lord gave Himself to give them eternal life.[2]

God's purpose of election is not fulfilled *apart* from the work of Christ but *through* it. He is the only Saviour that God has provided and election is 'for obedience and sprinkling of the blood of Jesus Christ'.[3] The doctrine of election requires Christ to love us, procure salvation for us through His death, and to apply His blood to us to cleanse us from all sin. Without the shedding of blood there is no forgiveness of sins and without the application of His blood to our consciences we cannot be cleansed.[4]

Election and evangelistic preaching

There are those who would argue that if God has elected whom He shall save, the preaching of the Gospel is rendered unnecessary. But this argument again fails to recognise that God has chosen to use means to accomplish His purposes — and one of these means is preaching. 'It pleased God through the foolishness of the message preached to save those who believe'. 'Of his own will he brought us forth by the word of truth'.[5]

The apostle Paul taught the doctrine of election but this did not hinder his evangelism. Rather it motivated it. Why was he willing to suffer so much for the cause of the Gospel? 'I endure all things for the sake of the elect that they may obtain the salvation that is in Christ Jesus'. Precisely because God had planned the salvation of innumerable people from every age and nation, Paul would suffer any deprivation to call them out through the preaching of the gospel.[6]

Nowhere does Scripture give more concentrated teaching on the doctrine of election than in Romans chapters nine to eleven. The sovereignty of God's grace and the freeness of God's mercy are extolled. Yet in the heart of those chapters Paul reminds his readers that men must call on the name of the Lord if they are to be saved. He asks, 'How then shall they call on him in whom they have not believed? And how shall they believe in him of whom they have not heard? And how shall they hear without a preacher? . . . Faith comes by hearing and hearing by the Word of God'.[7]

Unless the Gospel is preached men will not be saved. Just as men are not elected to salvation regardless of whether Christ died for them, even so they are not elected to salvation regardless of whether the Gospel is preached to them. The fact of election does not bypass means. Men are chosen to salvation *in* Christ and *through* preaching.

Election and the Holy Spirit

When Paul wrote to the Thessalonians he told them that he was confident of their election. Why? 'For our Gospel did not come to you in word only, but also in power, and in the Holy Spirit and in much assurance'.[8]

It is evident that it is possible for the Gospel to come in word 'only'. It is the same Gospel that is preached on other occasions — it is just as true as always — but something is lacking. The Spirit of God is not at work with the Word. Where He is, there the purpose of election is fulfilled because men and women are saved.

Later Paul explains this concept further. Paul

tells the Thessalonians that 'God from the beginning chose you to salvation through sanctification by the Spirit'.[9] When something is sanctified, it is set apart from its usual state and use. Paul has in view the great regenerating work of the Spirit by which men and women are distinguished from all others by having their hard, insensitive, stony hearts removed and replaced by hearts of flesh that pulsate with life and are sensitive and alive to God.[10]

This is the great work of the Spirit — the granting of spiritual rebirth to those dead in sin. This is a sovereign work of God. The Spirit is as free as the wind. He is not brought to men by their whim or their works but comes sovereignly to save such as have been chosen from the beginning.[11]

Just as men cannot be saved without the work of Christ and the preaching of the Gospel, so they cannot be saved without rebirth. To be born again is essential to salvation and is a consequence of the electing grace of God.

Election and faith

Paul reminds us that 'not all have faith' but that he is 'a servant of God and an apostle of Jesus Christ according to the faith of God's elect'.[12] Paul sees faith, true faith, the faith that receives salvation, as the possession of God's elect, for it is another means that God uses to save them. 'God from the beginning chose you for salvation through sanctification by the Spirit and belief in the truth'.[13]

The doctrine of election, therefore, does not

mean that we shall be saved whether or not we believe. God has chosen us to salvation *through* belief. The testimony of Scripture is clear. 'Without faith it is impossible to please God'. 'He who believes in him is not condemned, but he who does not believe is condemned already. He who believes in the Son has everlasting life: and he who does not believe the Son shall not see life, but the wrath of God abides on him'.[14] Belief is not some optional extra. It is woven into the very fabric of God's plan of salvation.

The message of the Gospel is not that we are saved by grace and nothing more needs to be said. It is 'by grace you have been saved through faith'.[15] If we do not believe in Christ we shall die in our sins and perish.

Conclusion

The doctrine of election does not mean that God has chosen who will be saved, come what may. Nor does it teach that God has made a plan of salvation full of 'ifs' and 'buts' which can be frustrated at any time. Rather it declares that God has determined *who* shall be saved and *how* they shall be saved. God has chosen them to salvation through the atoning work of Christ, the preaching of the Gospel, the regenerating work of the Holy Spirit and belief of the truth.

For further thought

1. To argue that preaching is unnecessary because God is in control of salvation is as absurd as arguing

that eating and breathing are unnecessary because
God is Lord of life and death.

2. What mistakes will be avoided with regard to the
doctrine of election if we compare the teaching of
Romans 8:28-30; 9:14-18 and 10:13-17?

1. *Ephesians 1:4.*
2. *Matthew 1:21; John 10:11; Ephesians 5:25; John 17:2.*
3. *Acts 4:12; 1 Peter 1:2.*
4. *Hebrews 9:15,22.*
5. *1 Corinthians 1:21; James 1:18.*
6. *2 Timothy 2:10; Revelation 7:9-10.*
7. *Romans 10:13-17.*
8. *1 Thessalonians 1:4-5.*
9. *2 Thessalonians 2:13.*
10. *Ezekiel 36:26.*
11. *John 3:8; 2 Thessalonians 2:13.*
12. *2 Thessalonians 3:2; Titus 1:1.*
13. *2 Thessalonians 2:13.*
14. *Hebrews 11:6; John 3:18,36.*
15. *Ephesians 2:8.*

Chapter 4

The Responsibilities

The Scriptures lay a number of responsibilities upon the elect. The first of these responsibilities is for their own peace of mind. The fact of a salvation planned in eternity might produce some fear in our hearts that we cannot be sure of God's purpose towards us. This could leave us in a state of tension and fear, but this need not be so.

Election and assurance

The apostle Peter wrote to the early Christians, 'be even more diligent to make your calling and election sure'.[1] Peter's desire was not, of course, that they should do something to reassure God that His plans would work! Rather it was that the Christians should be assured that they would not stumble and fall short of the promises of the Gospel. Peter assured them that they could know that they really were elect and called of God and that they would inherit what was promised in the Gospel.[2] To know this would, of course, bring them peace, joy and comfort.

Assurance of our election, calling and ultimate victory is given in a number of ways. Peter concentrates on assurance through the development of spiritual graces. Spiritual fruitfulness gives us the evidence of our election. This is the context of Peter's statement about election. It is also the teaching of our Lord, 'You did not choose me, but I chose you and appointed you that you should go and bear fruit and that your fruit should remain'.[3]

The principle is a simple one. Where the fruits of grace are found in the life, the evidence of election is present. Our Lord taught us to distinguish between the claims of men by the fruit that they produce in their lives.[4]

The root and power for developing assurance

In his reasoning, Peter assumes that his readers have faith. Such is the foundational nature of faith that we cannot be Christians without it. Not all men have faith but the elect do once they have been converted. It is by faith that we have come to know the Lord Jesus Christ.[5]

Through the knowledge of Jesus Christ we have all the resources that we need for our Christian life and the development of godliness. We believe in Christ and in Christ we have all that we need to meet every situation. Spiritual fruitfulness is within our grasp because Christ is all-sufficient to enable us to do the will of God. Rooted in faith and empowered in Christ we can add to our faith and see the fruit of our calling and election.[6]

The fruit that promotes assurance

Peter exhorts us to add seven things to faith. Firstly, we are to add to faith *virtue*.[7] Our faith is to be supplemented and evidenced by wholesome, virtuous goodness. Our faith in Christ is to increase and upgrade — even to transform — the moral quality of our lives. We are to be better people than we were and than the world is. We are not to give seeming credibility to the statement, 'All the nice people are outside of the church'. True faith has a quality that heightens our character; Zacchaeus, the thieving tax-collector, becomes the benevolent giver.[8]

To virtue is to be added *knowledge*.[9] The Bible is not anti-intellectual. It is not opposed to education. Ignorance is not a virtue. Biblical Christianity does not by-pass the mind but feeds it with truth that it might expand and grow. How can I claim to be elect if I do not want to know more about God and His truth? With what enthusiasm the Old Testament saints desired to know more and more of God's truth.[10] Do not cover up laziness by pleading you are, 'Just a simple Christian'.

Knowledge is to be accompanied by *self-control*.[11] The word means strength exercised against myself: self-mastery. It is a mark of the non-Christian that he is a slave of the devil, but the Christian is redeemed: freed from the Kingdom of Satan. He is Christ's freedman, so he is free to serve God not Satan, righteousness not sin. No more may we whine 'I must' when the tempter comes, but rather we resist the devil and he flees from us.[12]

This is not to say that our battle with sin and Satan is easy. The battles of our Christian lives can be hard and long. *Patient perseverance* is needed. Christianity is not about beginning a race but finishing it. When our hands begin to hang down and our knees begin to buckle we have need of encouragement and strengthening to go on. But God's elect do go on. They may fall but they always get up, for God preserves them, completing the work He has begun.[13]

To patient perseverance must be added *godliness*.[14] The idea is one of piety, spirituality. This is not a popular concept — even among Christians. How often the jibe is heard, 'Too heavenly-minded to be any earthly good'. Such a statement is an impossibility. Heavenly-mindedness — when the mind is set on things above and the heart is taken up with pleasing God — renders a person eminently useful. True piety is a rare commodity but a great comfort. It is inconceivable that a truly holy man shall perish.

When a person is pious and in love with God it also makes him *in love with God's people*. Love of God's people and assurance are closely linked. 'We know that we have passed from death to life because we love the brethren'. The apostle will not allow a division between love to God and love to our brother. 'Everyone who loves him who begat also love him who is begotten of him'.[15]

Nor is this love to be limited to God's people. Whereas all believers have a special call upon our love, all men have some call. We may not limit our 'neighbour' to those of the same race, group or even religion. If a Samaritan can love a Jew then the Christian, by grace, must love more deeply and more widely.[16]

Here then is the fruit that the Christian has been chosen to bear and by which he makes his calling and election sure. It is his responsibility to nurture these graces, but the power to do so comes from God and is rooted in his relationship with Christ.

For further thought

The first Epistle of John was written to believers so that they might *know* they had eternal life (1 John 5:12). What evidence of the 'faith of God's elect' does John mention that Peter omits?

1. 2 Peter 1:10.
2. 2 Peter 1:10-11.
3. 2 Peter 1:8-11; John 15:16.
4. Matthew 7:20.
5. 2 Peter 1:5; 2 Thessalonians 3;2; Titus 1:1; 2 Peter 1:8.
6. 2 Peter 1:3; Colossians 2:10; 2 Peter 1:5.
7. 2 Peter 1:5.
8. Luke 19:8-9.
9. 2 Peter 1:5.
10. Psalm 119:97; Job 23:12.
11. 2 Peter 1:6.
12. 2 Timothy 2:26; Colossians 1:13-14; 1 Corinthians 7:22; Romans 6:17-18; James 4:7.
13. 2 Peter 1:6; 1 Corinthians 9:24-27; Hebrews 12:12-13; Psalm 37:24; Philippians 1:6.
14. 2 Peter 1:6.
15. 2 Peter 1:7; 1 John 3:14; 5:1.
16. 2 Peter 1:7; Galatians 6:10; Luke 10:35-36; Colossians 3:12-14.

Chapter 5

The Present Consequences

Election has certain consequences for our status and position both in this life and the life to come. As well as responsibilities, our election grants us certain privileges which we need to remember.

Election and justification

There are undoubtedly many people who could bring accusations and criticisms against God's elect people. Satan could bring an account of all those times he has successfully tempted the Christian into sin. The Christian's enemies could no doubt find many grounds of criticism and even his friends would not be short of details of his sinful failing. Who among the world of Christians would be so foolish as to throw out our Lord's challenge, 'Which of you convicts me of sin'?[1]

More important, however, than the fact of these accusations, is the question: will God hear our accusers and bring in a verdict of condemnation against us for our sins? Paul assures us He shall not, for we are justified — declared righteous — in His sight. 'Who shall bring a charge against God's elect? It is God who justifies'. All the foreknown are predestined, called and justified.[2]

Of all the Scriptural writers none explain the doctrine of justification more clearly than Zechariah. In Zechariah 3:1-5 he envisages Joshua the High Priest — the God-appointed representative of God's people — standing in the presence of God. Satan is also present standing at his right hand — that is, in a position of strength and power, waiting to accuse him (v.1).

Before Satan can open his mouth to fulfil his familiar role as the accuser of the brethren,[3] God demands that he is rebuked. For the one Satan is about to accuse is chosen of God — elect — and plucked from the brink of destruction (v.2). Joshua the High Priest is the representative of God's elect and saved people.

It has to be confessed that Joshua in and of himself has no grounds on which to defend himself against Satan's accusations. His clothes are filthy. He is a sinner (v.3). God demands, however, the removal of his filthy clothes as a sign of the removal of his sin (v.4). This is the position of the elect, saved sinner. God has removed his sin. He has reckoned it to Christ. Its guilt has been attributed to God's Son. His death is the bearing of the sinner's punishment. The very sins of which Satan would accuse him have now been removed and attributed to another.[4]

There is, however, more. Joshua's filthy clothes have not been removed to leave him unclothed. His salvation does not consist merely in the removal of sin to return him to Adamic innocence. New, clean clothes are also put upon him (vs. 4-5). Not only is sin removed, but the righteousness of Christ is given and attributed to him also. He is not simply, therefore, sin-free but he is positively good. The goodness of Christ — His status — is granted to the believer. This is the righteousness held out in the Gospel in which Paul delighted and gloried. Not only does God reckon our sin to Christ but He reckons Christ's righteousness to us.[5]

It is significant that Zechariah does not record one word of accusation passing Satan's lips. He is silenced by the blood and righteousness of Christ. He can bring no charge against God's elect because they are declared righteous in the sight of God. Only if a fault could be found in the righteousness of Christ could a word of accusation be allowed.

Election and apostasy

The power of false teaching in the world should never be under-estimated. Behind the lies of men and their false teachings is the power of Satan himself. He is the father of lies, and a constant stream of heresy and deception flows from his lips. He is crafty and scheming, and baits his hook well to catch the unsuspecting.[6]

Christians are not exempt from the attacks and temptations of Satan. A true Christian can resist the truth as Peter did when he opposed the death of our Lord and in so doing became the tool of Satan. He can even be cowardly and let our Lord down at the crucial time as the disciples did when they forsook Him at His arrest. A true Christian can even deny Christ with oaths when under pressure in order to

save his own life. A true child of God may be led
astray for all sorts of reasons, and like the Galatians
of old, 'toy' with another Gospel.[7]

The backslidings of a Christian are a sad reality.
The path back can be long and bitter. The Christian's toying with error can be very dangerous and
be a great hindrance to his Christian growth.[8] But a
true Christian — one of God's elect — may not, and
will not, be so deceived as to desert Christ entirely
for a false Christ. Our Lord teaches, 'For false
Christs and false prophets will arise and show great
signs and wonders so as to deceive, if possible, the
very elect'.[9] The key words are 'if possible'. The aim
of the false teachers is to deceive the very elect if
that were possible. Thank God it is not!

The elect cannot totally be drawn away from
Christ because, where God has begun a work, He
completes it. The hand of God has closed around
the sheep for whom Christ died. It is beyond the
ability of any to break the grip of God and to cause
those in His hand to perish. The apostle Paul declares his great persuasion. He surveys the universe
physical and spiritual; history yesterday, today and
tomorrow, and he finds that no-one and nothing
'shall be able to separate us from the love of God
which is in Christ Jesus our Lord'.[10]

The elect may fall and fail, deny, wander and
backslide but they do not shrink back to be des-
troyed for they have believed unto the saving of the
soul and are secure in the hands of God.[11]

For further thought

Are the following two statements accurate or overstated?

1. In Christ the believer is as beautiful and sin free in God's sight as Christ himself.

2. The glorified spirits of dead Christians in heaven are more happy but not more secure than Christians on earth with regard to their salvation.

1. *John 8:46.*
2. *Romans 8:33,29.*
3. *Revelation 12:10.*
4. *2 Corinthians 5:21; 1 Peter 2:24; Isaiah 53:5.*
5. *Romans 3:21-22; Philippians 3:8-9; 2 Corinthians 5:21.*
6. *1 Timothy 4:1-3; John 8:44; 2 Corinthians 11:13-14.*
7. *Matthew 16:22-23, 26:56, 69-75; Galatians 1:6,9.*
8. *Galatians 5:7.*
9. *Matthew 24:24.*
10. *Philippians 1:6; John 10:28-29; Romans 8:30-39.*
11. *Hebrews 10:39.*

Chapter 6

The Future Consequences

God's preservation of His elect people has a defi-
nite end in view. Paul desires the elect to obtain
salvation 'with eternal glory'. God's people are
foreknown, predestined, called, justified and, to
emphasise its certainty it is placed in the past tense,
'glorified'.[1] The glorification of the elect is the end
in view, but what is glorification?

Election and the presence of Christ

In his High Priestly prayer (John 17) our Lord was
particularly concerned for those whom the Father
had given Him — His elect people (vs. 2,6,9,10). He
had given them the knowledge of the Father which
is eternal life (vs. 2-10). He prayed for their preservation (vs. 11-16), their sanctification (vs. 17-19),
their unity (vs. 20-23) and their glorification (v. 24).
Our Lord's prayer was, 'Father I desire that they
also whom you gave me may be with me where I
am'. He desired their presence with Him in the
presence of His Father. Our Lord wants His people
to be with Him.

To be with Christ is the very thing that trans-
forms the Christian's attitude to death. Paul knew

the responsibilities and needs of the hour but pre-ferred to depart life 'and be with Christ which is far better'. To be absent from this body which is so affected by sin is 'to be present with the Lord'.[2]

To be with Christ is not simply the Christian's hope in His death. It is the whole hope of the coming of Christ and the resurrection. The Christian's comfort is that when the Christian dead of all ages shall have been raised they shall meet the Lord in the air, and 'we shall always be with the Lord'.[3]

Then the absent, invisible Lord shall be hidden from us no longer. Faith shall give way to sight. High among the blessings of eternity shall be this: 'they shall see his face'.[4] The veil shall be removed. The Lord shall be there and the joy of all His people.

Election and victory

At the end of our Lord's earthly ministry, He contemplated the restoration of the glory He had with the Father in eternity. After His death He explained His ascension as entering 'into His glory'. His ascension and sitting down at the right hand of God is referred to as His glorification.[5] Thus His glorification was His day of victory and triumph when He ascended and sat down on the throne of His Father.

The Christian also shall be glorified. He too shall enter into victory. Our Lord promised, 'To him who overcomes I will grant to sit with me on my throne, as I also overcame and sat down with my Father on his throne'.[6] As Christ completed His work and sat down in triumph so shall we.

Is Christ the Son of God? The Christian is a son of

God by adoption. Is Christ the heir of God? The Christian is a joint heir with Christ. Is Christ the heir of all things? All things are the inheritance of the Christian in Christ.[7]

Whatever their present struggles, the chosen people of God have victory ahead of them. They shall ascend to be with Christ. They shall be enthroned with Christ. They shall reign with Him.[8]

Election and Christlikeness

Of all the aspects of glorification perhaps none is more amazing than that God has predestined His elect, 'to be conformed to the image of his Son'.[9] The blue-print for God's people eternally is Christ. They shall be made like Him. They shall reflect His moral character.

The doctrine of justification is amazing enough! Sinners are reckoned and treated as if as righteous as Christ, but Paul's doctrine in Romans is breathtaking. Vile, hell-deserving sinners shall not only be reckoned as righteous but shall be *made* righteous. This is the real Biblical doctrine of entire sanctification. This is the amazing purpose of election. No wonder John wrote, 'Behold what manner of love the Father has bestowed on us that we should be called children of God! ... It has not yet been revealed what we shall be, but we know that when he is revealed we shall be like him'.[10]

The desire of every Christian's heart to be more and more like Jesus shall be fulfilled. For the endless ages of eternity the elect people of God shall have their character conformed to His character. Here is disclosed the great purpose of God in election: to people eternity with an innumerable host of the redeemed, all of whom reflect in their character the unparalleled moral beauty of Christ. In this way Christ shall have His proper place — 'the place of pre-eminence'.[11]

To God be all the Glory.

For further thought

1. The wonder of eternity is found in the presence of Christ there. But in addition everyone there will reflect the same moral character as Christ. God's purpose is to people eternity with sinners made to be like His Son.

2. What is it that makes the present labours of the Christian worthwhile? (1 Corinthians 15:50-59).

1. *2 Timothy 2:10; Romans 8:30.*
2. *Philippians 1:23; 2 Corinthians 5:8.*
3. *1 Thessalonians 4:17-18.*
4. *Revelation 22:4.*
5. *John 17:5; Luke 24:26; John 7:39.*
6. *Revelation 3:21.*
7. *Galatians 4:4-5; Romans 8:16-17; Hebrews 1:2; 1 Corinthians 3:21-23.*
8. *2 Timothy 2:12.*
9. *Romans 8:29.*
10. *1 John 3:1-2.*
11. *Colossians 1:10.*

Section Two

Human Responsibility

Chapter 7

Robots?

When our forefathers, at the end of the nineteenth century and the beginning of the twentieth, began to phantasise about a distant scientific age of amazing men and machines, they could hardly have expected many of the stunning advances of the modern world. The space station and the shuttle, the computer and the word processor are taken for granted, even by most schoolboys. Numerous books have appeared on how to programme computers, the types of programme and the results that can be attained through their use. It seems that computers and robots can be devised to do almost anything. We have a world full of pre-programmed machines, mindless servants doing the will of the master-race, the programmers, who determine the material to be fed into the machines.

Increasingly this model of a world of machines controlled by their programmers is being taken across and imposed on society. Religions, philosophies and world-views vie with one another to explain history, society, behaviour and life-style in accordance with the idea of determinism. This means that everything that happens is somehow pre-arranged in such a way that man can no longer be considered responsible for his actions. All human freedom is an illusion. As the once popular song said, 'What will be, will be'.

Some Moslems have a theological fatalism. They see all things bound up in the will of Allah and that their fulfilment is inevitable. Consequently, in some parts of the world among simple peoples it is not unknown for Moslems to walk across a street of traffic looking neither to the right nor to the left in accordance with the principle that if Allah has willed death it will occur and if Allah has willed survival it will happen! No amount of road safety practice can affect his will.

In Western societies, however, the approach of determinism is usually more sophisticated. Man is viewed as a chemical machine that is wholly material. His behaviour is determined not by fate but by his genetic constitution. Character is controlled by genes, and behaviour is simply the outworking of this genetic chemistry. What we are, is determined by our genes, and, therefore, there is no real responsibility, only activity. The immoral person is defined as a person who is genetically 'over-sexed'; the perverted person is simply genetically orientated in a different way to most other people. Even to speak in terms of morality, right or wrong, good or bad, becomes inappropriate because a man is determined in his behaviour by his genes, not by his decisions.

Yet others emphasise environmental factors. It is not merely argued that bad housing, unemployment, political instability, examples of violence have an effect upon behaviour — for most people would accept that they do to some degree — but it is contended that these things determine behaviour and remove personal responsibility.

In the classroom the teacher is told that he cannot write a truthful report on a naughty child because the child's naughtiness is a product of his home conditions. Bad homes create bad children. In the court-room the lawyer pleads that unemployment led the youth to violence and that society and not the violent youth is to blame. This type of argument is popular and carries weight, particularly among those who have what they would consider to be 'enlightened' views.

It is also a favourite ploy of the enemies of the truth of the sovereignty of God (which was explained in the first half of this book in relation to election) to suggest that the Biblical doctrine of predestination and the doctrine of fatalism are virtually identical. It is argued that if God is sovereign man cannot be responsible. People like Judas are viewed as victims of Divine plans. God planned that Judas had to betray Christ. Therefore, like it or not, Judas was obliged to be the betrayer. Poor Judas! This caricature of the sovereignty of God and the responsibility of Judas will, however, find no place in Scripture.

The Scriptures do not view men as robots. There is a recognition of sinfulness in human nature from conception. Circumstances are seen as having an effect upon behaviour. Too much wealth is presented as a temptation to arrogance, too little wealth as a temptation to theft. Parental restraint, or lack of it, is seen to have its effects on children either in their discipline or their destruction. God is asserted to be sovereign, doing His will without being able to be criticised or restrained both among angels and among men.[1] But none of these facts is ever used in Scripture to excuse human sin or to suggest than men are not responsible for their behaviour. There are robots in this world and there are men, but men are not robots.

For further thought

1. How much would you blame the media for other people's violence?
2. Are parents responsible for the behaviour of their children?
3. Does the military plea, 'I was only obeying orders', free the serviceman from guilt?

1. Psalm 51:5; Proverbs 30:8-9; 22:15; 1 Samuel 3:13; Daniel 4:35.

Chapter 8

Adam — A Responsible Creature

The Scriptures do not present man as a product of a hit-and-miss process of evolution originating by chance. Man is seen as a creation of God, created by a specific Triune decision as an act of special creation. The combination of the dust of the ground and the breath of God produced man made in the image of God.[1]

There have been many different understandings of what it is for man to be created in God's image. Some concentrate on the Genesis statement that God created man in His image and created them male and female.[2] They see the image of God as primarily concerned with relationships. Just as within God there are relationships between the Father, the Son and the Holy Spirit, so God created man to have and develop relationships. Man reflects God's image as he lives and works in society.

Others focus attention on the command of God to man to fill the earth, subdue it and exercise dominion over creation.[3] Man reflects the image of God in the way that he rules and controls the creation in and over which he has been placed.

In defining the image of God, others have taken

the lead from the New Testament use of the concept rather than limiting themselves to Genesis. The renewal of the image of God in man through Christ is presented in terms of knowledge, righteousness and holiness.[4] The image of God in man is seen in his being a rational and spiritual being, in terms of his ability to reason and his morality.

Whichever of these definitions of the image of God is adopted, or even if we accept all three, the significant point is that each requires man to be viewed not as a mindless robot obeying his programme but as a responsible being, thinking, asking, reacting, involved, creative and responsive within God's world. None of the definitions of the image of God support the chemical machine view of man.

It is also evident that in His treatment of Adam, God expected him to exercise initiatives, to have responses and to accept responsibilities. Duties were given to Adam to fulfil. He was to work in Eden and care for it. He was to name and define the animal creation. He was to propagate his species and fill the earth and bring it under his control as his servant. Supremely he was to remember his creaturehood and that there is a God who rules over him. This rule of God was to be symbolised by the forbidding to him of the fruit of a particular tree. Disobedience to this command would lead to sure and inevitable disaster.[5]

The giving of command, the setting out of duties, and the threat of penalties for disobedience all emphasise that Adam was treated by God as a responsible creature. There was no inherent inevitability about his fall into sin. He knew his duty. He knew the consequences of disobedience. He chose to disobey.

Neither in the description of Adam's fall into sin in the Genesis narrative, nor anywhere else in Scripture, is there a plea for mitigating circumstances. The poet Milton might suggest that Adam had to sin once Eve had, otherwise he would have been unchivalrous, but such ideas have more to do with poetic fancy than with solid fact!

There is in Scripture a deliberate and emphasised contrast between Eve's sin and Adam's. The Genesis account traces step by step the way in which Satan enticed Eve into sin. Whenever the Scripture refers to this there is an emphasis upon the influence and activity of Satan. By his cunning and subtlety Satan led Eve astray. Eve was deceived and became a sinner.[6]

In contrast there is no mention of Adam's being deceived. Indeed, he was said not to be deceived. There is no indication that Satan did any preparatory work on Adam. Genesis boldly states that when Eve offered him the forbidden fruit he ate it. His sin is seen as a clear act of rebellion. He is clearly regarded as the person responsible for the sin and its consequences in just the same way as Christ is regarded as responsible for providing salvation. Adam sinned, transgressed and brought the consequences of his sin on his descendants. In taking the fruit he was not fulfilling bad programming like an automaton, he was sinning, transgressing and *disobeying*.[7] He was doing what God had told him *not* to do. The responsibility for his sin is fully his. God asked Adam what he had done because the action and responsibility were *entirely* Adam's. He had not sinned because of chemical imbalance, genetic distortion, environmental conditioning, or Divine force. He had freely disobeyed and was responsible for what he had done.

For further thought
1. What do Genesis 3:8-13 suggest about where Adam and Eve put the blame for their sin?
2. What do Genesis 3:8-19 suggest about where God put the blame for Adam and Eve's sin?

1. *Genesis 2:7; 1:26.*
2. *Genesis 1:27.*
3. *Genesis 1:28-30.*
4. *Colossians 3:10; Ephesians 4:24.*
5. *Genesis 2:15-20.*
6. *Genesis 3:1-6; 2 Corinthians 11:3; 1 Timothy 2:14.*
7. *1 Timothy 2:14; Genesis 3:6; Romans 5:12-21.*

Chapter 9

Sinners — Responsible Creatures

There are undoubtedly differences between ourselves, as descendants of Adam, and Adam. We were not created in a perfect world with a sin-free nature from which we rebelled into sin. We are bearers of the sinful nature of our ancestors, and from conception have sin in our natures. Our world is full of the consequences of sin.[1] It might, therefore, be argued that we are victims of our own ancestry and sinful natures — victims rather than those who can be held responsible for our actions.

Again, however, Scripture will not allow us to excuse ourselves and shift the blame for our sins to Adam or our natures. There are four very clear lines of teaching in Scripture which declare that God considers us responsible creatures. They have to do with creation, conscience, the Gospel and the Day of Judgment.

1. Responsibility and creation

Men often desire to leave some lasting memorial of themselves so that they will be remembered by the generations to come. In various lands there are 'follies' displaying the eccentricities, carelessness and sheer luxuriance of their makers. On the other hand, there are monuments, inventions, works of art, etc. which declare the greatness, ingenuity and skill of their creators.

According to Scripture, God has left himself a lasting memorial. It is the whole universe. Among the nations of the earth in every land this great monument is seen. The heavens, the sun, all created things are a memorial to God.[2]

The universe is not a folly but a grand display of the glory of God.[3] The glory of something is that which gives it its significance and attracts attention to it. Every work of art reveals it had a creator, declares his skill or lack of it and earns either praise or criticism from its admirers. In the same way the universe bears an eloquent testimony to God. It declares His existence before it was created, His eternity, for it is self-evident that the artist must exist before His work of art! It declares His skill or power in creation. What a great God He must be to have made such a complex, varied universe like this! It declares His worthiness to be glorified and praised. Who else could have made a universe where every finger-print and snow-flake is different from the others? The creation reveals the eternal power and Godhead of God its creator.[4]

The witness of God to Himself in His creation is not passive and static. God does not wait for man to look at creation and reach clever conclusions. He is actively making Himself known, bearing witness to Himself, so that the things about God revealed in creation are plain to men — to their sight — and in them — in their minds.[5]

The Scriptures have no time for the atheist's contention that there is not enough evidence for believing in God, or the agnostic's idea that we cannot be sure if there is a God. The Scriptures tell us that just as the existence of a painting declares clearly the existence of a painter, so God is clearly telling us of His existence — and more — through the creation.[6]

Such is the clarity of God's self-revelation in creation that failure on the part of any human being to recognise the existence of their creator, His power, and His worthiness to be worshipped is said to be inexcusable. It provokes God to anger because it is a holding back of truth about God that is obvious. It is a deliberate refusal to face self-evident, God-supported facts.[7]

God holds us responsible to glorify Him as our Creator and feels able to punish us justly for failing to do so. We may not plead ignorance of God, only a wilful rejection or ignoring of His witness to Himself. The day of Christ's wrath is, therefore, firstly against those who do not know God, for such ignorance is culpable.[8]

For further thought

1. 'The witness to God in creation is irrelevant in a non-agricultural society'. Do you agree?
2. What does the witness of creation mean for the idea that only the Gospel rejector can be under God's wrath?

1. *Genesis 5:1-3; 3:14-19; Psalm 51:5.*
2. *Psalm 19:1-6; Romans 1:20.*
3. *Psalm 19:1.*
4. *Romans 1:20.*
5. *Romans 1:19.*
6. *Romans 1:19-20.*
7. *Romans 1:18-20.*
8. *2 Thessalonians 1:8*

2. *Responsibility and conscience*

Not only does every man have a witness to God outside of himself but also inside. Our inner sense of right and wrong, our intuitive ideas of justice and injustice, our feelings of concern about certain things we propose to do and guilt about some of the things we have done; these are all part and parcel of our human constitution. Knowing what is basically right and fundamentally wrong is not just something that we are taught.

The Old Testament prophets had no difficulty in condemning the pagan nations surrounding Israel for their acts of inhumanity and unnatural cruelty. The pagan nations were not considered excused from their sins or without responsibility for their barbarities because they had never heard of the revelation of the Law of God to Moses.

Amos condemned Syria, Philistia, Ammon and Moab and promised them the judgment of God because of their excessive barbarity. He promised wrath on Tyre and Edom for their unfaithful, unbrotherly conduct towards Judah.[1] They were pagans — devoid of the revelation given to Israel — but they were neither innocent nor lacking in responsibility for their actions.

The condemnation of pagans is based on the fact that although they do not have God's written law as found in the Bible they do have 'the work of the Law written in their hearts'.[2] By the 'work of the Law' Paul means the basic principles or ideas that are enshrined and detailed in the Law of God. Our Lord taught that the two principles on which the Law of God hangs are the need of man to love God and his need to love his fellow human beings.[3] All men are created with this sense of religious and humanitarian duty within them.

This 'work of the Law' or moral sense has two allies. The first is the conscience, which prods the moral sense of duty or reminds it of failure. The second is the thought processes of the mind by which we think out what we feel we ought to do or ought not to have done.[4] This internal trio work together to render us accountable to God.

There is considerable emphasis in Scripture on keeping a clear or good conscience as a goal in life. There are also warnings against persisting in sin and error and thereby rendering the conscience insensitive and corrupt.[5] Just as men may resist the witness of creation to God, so they may resist the testimony of their conscience that they are accountable to God, but opposing the truth does not change it! The feeling that men sometimes have at the back of their minds that gnaws away at their self-confidence, is well-grounded. 'You won't get away with it in the end', a voice seems to say. The witness of that 'voice' is true. The secrets of men will be judged.[6]

For further thought

1. Is it truthful or accurate to speak of 'the innocent heathen'?
2. What are the limits of the truth revealed by conscience?

1. *Amos 1:3-2:3.*
2. *Romans 2:15.*
3. *Matthew 22:36-40.*
4. *Romans 2:15.*
5. *Acts 24:16; 1 Timothy 1:5; 4:2; Titus 1:15.*
6. *Romans 2:12-16.*

3. Responsibility and the Gospel

The revelation of the existence and character of God that all men have in creation and their own moral constitution is greatly supplemented wherever the Gospel of the Lord Jesus Christ is preached. The ideas of God as eternal Creator, powerful, worthy of worship, and a moral Judge are enhanced and developed by the idea of God as gracious, merciful, loving and saving.

The Gospel is, of course, a proclamation of facts. The Gospel preacher declares what God the Father has planned for the salvation of men, how God the Son has procured that salvation and how God the Holy Spirit applies it. The Gospel is fundamentally good news about the great saving activities of a Triune God.

To be Biblical, however, Gospel preaching cannot simply proclaim what God has done. It also has to proclaim what men must do to benefit from the salvation proclaimed. The proclamation of the Gospel has to do with human duty and, therefore, human responsibility, not solely Divine action.

Attached to the preaching of the Gospel and as an integral part of it there are Divine commands to the sinner to respond in a particular way. The kings of the earth who lead the people against the rule of Christ are commanded to serve Him and kiss Him — to pay Him homage and show Him allegiance. They are commanded to cease from rebellion.[1]

The hostile crowd who questioned what our Lord was teaching, and from whom He had to hide Himself away because of the obstinancy of its unbelief, was nevertheless commanded to walk in the light and believe in the light while it had opportunity.[2]

Our Lord required His disciples to preach repentance and forgiveness among the nations. They interpreted this as a Divine command to all men, everywhere, to repent.[3] Repentance is a duty laid on men by the Gospel. All who hear the Gospel are responsible to repent.

The duties placed on man by the hearing of the Gospel are not always framed in terms of commands. Sometimes they are in the form of invitations and passionate pleading,[4] but the hearers are responsible for their response.

Unbelief is presented in the Scriptures as a sin. The Holy Spirit convicts the world of sin — and the sin in view is unbelief in Christ. To be unbelieving is to be in a state of condemnation. In the present, God judges men, handing them over to delusions and lies when they will not believe the truth but delight in unrighteousness. In the future Christ's wrath is not only against those who know not God but also against those who do not obey the Gospel.[5]

When the Jewish people would not listen to our Lord as He called her to follow Him, she was held responsible and brought under judgment. The armies that surrounded Jerusalem in AD70 razed it to the ground, and scattered its survivors throughout the world, were tools of judgment against a people held responsible for rejecting Christ.[6] The Gospel holds out salvation but it holds its rejectors responsible for the judgment that comes on them.

For further thought

1. Does God view immorality or Gospel rejection as most serious (Matthew 11:20-24)?
2. What can we learn about the responsibility of the Gospel hearer from Acts 13:38-48?

1. *Psalm 2.*
2. *John 12:34-36.*
3. *Luke 24:47; Acts 17:30.*
4. *Matthew 11:28-30; 2 Corinthians 5:20.*
5. *John 16:8-9; 3:18; 2 Thessalonians 2:11-12; 1:7-8.*
6. *Matthew 23:37-38; Luke 19:41-44.*

4. Responsibility and Judgment Day

We have already seen that man has within him a nagging conviction that he will not get away with his undiscovered sins. This sense of foreboding points to a day of reckoning. In both the Old and New Testaments there is the expectancy of a Day of Judgment — a day for which men ought to prepare.[1] The world has often consigned the 'Prepare to meet thy God' concept to the bill-boards of the lunatic fringe but it may not be so lightly dismissed.

There is a very marked relationship in the Scriptures between behaviour and Divine judgment. The Patriarchs of old had to learn that God is the Judge of all the earth and does what is right. Therefore, they witnessed the saving of righteous Lot and the destruction of evil Sodom.[2] Isaiah proclaimed that it would be well for the righteous but threatened woes to the wicked. Their respective deeds would come back on their heads either for blessing or cursing.[3]

Our Lord held before His hearers a Day of Judgment when an account would have to be rendered for every idle word.[4] Paul the Apostle often spoke of receiving back from God in reward or punishment that which had been done. Our life-style or works have their consequences and will be expected to be explained before God and duly vindicated or condemned.[5]

Just as Cain, when he killed his brother Abel, and Adam, when he ate the forbidden fruit, were asked what they had done — all the weight of responsibility being thrown on them — so every sinner will appear before his Judge to have the secrets of his heart revealed, judged and rewarded.

Of course, every single factor will be taken into account. One of the great problems of present human judgment is that it depends on what it sees and hears. It has not got enough facts to lay hold on. It cannot penetrate deeply enough. Therefore, we often have to suspend judgment, knowing that all

the facts will be revealed only when the Lord comes
and that His judgment alone is entirely righteous.[6]
But on that Day 'the truth will out' and judgment be
declared.

There is no hiding from God's judgment, no
possibility of escape. The Bible pictures the terror
that the arrival of that Day will bring. Every attempt
will be made to avoid the unavoidable but without
hope of success. We will then be held fully accountable and responsible for all that we have done.[7]
When that Day dawns all will know that it was not
the idea of religious eccentrics but the Day planned
by Almighty God.

We need to let these facts sink in. God our
Creator Judge holds us responsible and accountable for our reaction to His revelation in creation,
the conscience, and the Gospel and for all our other
activities and reactions. When all due weight is
given to all the factors that influence us and all the
pressures that are on us, we are *still* responsible,
accountable creatures, and neither robots nor victims.

For further thought

1. What effect should Judgment Day have on the
complaint that 'life is not fair'?
2. Is it wrong to use fear to restrain evil?

1. *Amos 4:12; Hebrews 9:27.*
2. *Genesis 18:25; 19.*
3. *Isaiah 3:10-11.*
4. *Matthew 12:36-37.*
5. *Romans 2:5-16.*
6. *1 Corinthians 4:3-5; Isaiah 11:3-4.*
7. *Revelation 6:12-17; Amos 5:18-19.*

Chapter 10

Human Responsibility and Divine Sovereignty

In the first half of this book we sought to address the subject of the sovereignty of God in salvation — His sovereign election of some to life eternal. In this second half the responsibility of men to believe, receive and obey all that God has revealed has been demonstrated. The question still remains of the relationship between Divine sovereignty and human responsibility.

An obvious case in point is that of Judas Iscariot. The betrayal of our Lord effected by Judas is clearly stated to be a result of the Divine plan. It had been determined by God. In the very same verse (Luke 22:22) as woe is pronounced and blame attached to the betrayer, God is presented as having planned the act for which Judas was held responsible.

There have been many attempts to explain the nature of the relationship between Divine plan and human responsibility. None of them has been particularly successful because they have invariably led to either a diminution of Divine sovereignty in order to maximise human responsibility or an over-emphasis on Divine decree that virtually cancels human responsibility.

The real answer to the problem is probably to be

found in antinomy. We have antinomy when two truths are held together in tension without their exact relationship to each other being able to be fully explained. After all, the Bible does not call us to believe only what we can fully understand. It calls us to receive what is revealed and to leave what is unrevealed to God. Our understanding can never be the measure of Divine activity because there is a real difference between our thoughts and His, our ways and His ways.[1]

Nor is antinomy something peculiar to these two doctrines. It is part of the genius of Biblical Christianity to leave us with tension at the heart of every major doctrine. Heresy or false teaching invariably arises from the desire to be rid of problems, and involve the denial of some facet of the truth.

Antinomy is at the heart of the Biblical doctrine of God. He is three: Father, Son and Holy Spirit. He is also one. Heretics become either tritheists denying His unity, or unitarians denying His persons. The Biblical doctrine, however, rejects the either/or approach for the idea of both/and. No-one can *exactly* explain the relationship of the three to the one but then should we expect to understand God fully?

Antinomy is necessary to the Biblical doctrine of the Person of Christ. He is fully God — and as such is worshipped. He is fully man — and as such has a ministry of fellow-feeling and sympathy. Heretics have either denied His Deity or His real humanity. The Bible asserts both. When heretics cry, 'It is not logical', our retort must be, 'But is it Biblical'?

In the same way those who reject antinomy in relation to sovereignty and responsibility usually end up downgrading one or the other. Some in over-asserting sovereignty destroy the cutting edge of Gospel preaching that requires sinners to face up to the duties and responsibilities placed on them. Some in asserting responsibility reduce God to a dethroned vassal subservient to the human will, and unable to decide anything until man allows Him. The truth of antinomy avoids both. God is sovereign; man is responsible. Both are true; both are to be preached, believed and obeyed.

For further thought

1. 'Christianity is not unreasonable, but reason cannot fully explain or understand it'.
2. A murderer explained to a judge, 'I couldn't help it, I was predestined to do it'. The judge retorted, 'And I am predestined to hang you'. Were they right or wrong?

1. *Deuteronomy 29:29; Isaiah 55:8-9.*

Chapter 11

Human Responsibility and Human Ability

It is a common mistake to confuse human *responsibility* to believe and obey God and human *ability* to do so, but there is an important difference. The law of the land may forbid its citizens to get drunk or take hard drugs, and decree penalties for disobedience. All citizens are responsible to obey. When a sober citizen drinks too much or takes too many drugs he may become a drunkard and finally an alcoholic, or drug-dependent and ultimately a junkie. The fact that he has become enslaved to drink or drugs does not change his responsibility to avoid drunkenness or drug addiction, but it certainly affects his ability to avoid these. He is under the enslaving, destroying control of his habit — responsible to keep clear of its dangers but unable to avoid its attractions.

The same is true of every man or woman in relation to God. The fact that we are sinners does not reduce our responsibility to worship the God revealed in creation, to obey our inner sense or moral duty, to believe the Gospel and to prepare for Judgment Day, but the fact of our sinfulness destroys our ability to do these things. Left to ourselves in our sin we cannot worship God acceptably, we will disregard conscience. The Gospel will be foolishness to us and eternity will be pushed out of our thoughts.

The Biblical doctrine of human inability to fulfil our responsibilities to God makes sombre reading. Only when a black man can turn his skin white and a leopard get rid of his spots can those accustomed to doing evil do good. None of us is righteous — up to God's standards; none is good; none has spiritual understanding or perception. The Gospel seems foolish or offensive to us. None of us would seek the true God left to himself. Our hearts are at enmity with God. We do not want to obey God or be subject to Him. We cannot love God or respond to His ways because we love darkness rather than light. Sin is more attractive to us than salvation.[1]

It is in this light that it is impossible to speak of the freedom of the human will to obey God. The will enslaved by sin is no more free than the will enslaved by drink or drugs. The will is in bondage to its own love for sin. Left to himself man has no heart nor desire for God and His salvation.

The desperate state of man is not, however, without remedy. He may be enslaved by his sin, careless about eternity and spiritually dead, but God is a God who raises the dead! Men are responsible to worship God, obey God, believe the Gospel and prepare for eternity, but cannot because of the hold of sin upon them. The world with its fashions, the devil with his temptations, and the flesh with its lusts rules in a context of spiritual death. But God in mercy and love makes the spiritual dead live.[2]

This spiritual life is a sovereign gift of God. This is the rebirth that our Lord required and it is given by God with as little predictability as the blowing of the wind.[3] But where it occurs the enslaving power of the world, the flesh and the devil is broken, the heart is changed, the will is freed, faith is produced and the blessings promised in the Gospel become ours.[4]

We stand before God as responsible creatures. We live before God as enslaved sinners. We need to be given spiritual life by God or we will perish, the victims of our own sinful life-style. Therefore, let us face the responsibilities the Gospel lays upon us and let us cry out to the living God to do for us what we cannot and will not do if left to ourselves.

For further thought

1. A boy without legs is not able to come downstairs for breakfast — he is naturally unable. A boy who loves his bed and wants to go on sleeping is not able to come downstairs for breakfast — he is morally unable. Are sinners naturally or morally unable to come to God?
2. Have you faced up to your responsibilities and cried to God for salvation?

1. *Jeremiah 13:23; Romans 3:10-13; 1 Corinthians 1:18, 23; Romans 8:7-8; John 3:19.*
2. *Ephesians 2:1-5.*
3. *John 3:8.*
4. *Ephesians 2:1-10.*